YOUR KNOWLEDGE HAS VALUE

- We will publish your bachelor's and master's thesis, essays and papers

- Your own eBook and book - sold worldwide in all relevant shops

- Earn money with each sale

Upload your text at www.GRIN.com and publish for free

Bibliographic information published by the German National Library:

The German National Library lists this publication in the National Bibliography; detailed bibliographic data are available on the Internet at http://dnb.dnb.de .

This book is copyright material and must not be copied, reproduced, transferred, distributed, leased, licensed or publicly performed or used in any way except as specifically permitted in writing by the publishers, as allowed under the terms and conditions under which it was purchased or as strictly permitted by applicable copyright law. Any unauthorized distribution or use of this text may be a direct infringement of the author s and publisher s rights and those responsible may be liable in law accordingly.

Imprint:

Copyright © 2016 GRIN Verlag, Open Publishing GmbH
Print and binding: Books on Demand GmbH, Norderstedt Germany
ISBN: 9783668575431

This book at GRIN:

http://www.grin.com/en/e-book/381146/great-theorists-jean-piaget-versus-lev-vygotsky

Patrick Kimuyu

Great Theorists. Jean Piaget versus Lev Vygotsky

GRIN Publishing

GRIN - Your knowledge has value

Since its foundation in 1998, GRIN has specialized in publishing academic texts by students, college teachers and other academics as e-book and printed book. The website www.grin.com is an ideal platform for presenting term papers, final papers, scientific essays, dissertations and specialist books.

Visit us on the internet:

http://www.grin.com/

http://www.facebook.com/grincom

http://www.twitter.com/grin_com

GREAT THEORISTS: JEAN PIAGET VERSUS LEV VYGOTSKY

Name: Patrick K. Kimuyu

Introduction

Child development appears to be one of the most studied phenomena of human development, especially with regard to cognitive and biopsychology. In the nineteenth century, child development attracted both philosophers and psychologists and, this can be attributed to the intrinsic nature of the topic because; it encompassed numerous mysteries and controversy. Ordinarily, childhood is usually accompanied by transient developmental changes, which are governed by the child's inherent biological characteristics and the ambient social conditions in the neighborhood. As such, the phenomena of child's development can be approached from diverse perspectives and, this was the case in the early nineteenth century when a number of prominent scholars studied the issue and hypothesized different theories on child development. For instance, Jean Piaget and Lev Vygotsky were among the most prominent scholars who contributed significantly to the advancement of studies on child development through postulating reliable theories although their principal postulates exhibit variations. Slanders (2009) remarks, "Swiss philosopher Jean Piaget and Russian psychologist Lev Vygotsky each developed their own ideas of child development" (par. 1). Nevertheless, theories developed by these two theorists have been useful to teachers and parents in enhancing learning and growth of children. Slanders (2009), reaffirms, "Piaget and Vygotsky contributed heavily toward the field of child development. Even though, their theories are fundamentally different, teachers and parents can incorporate both as they help their students and children learn and grow" (par. 3). Therefore, this research paper will discuss the significant similarities and differences between Jean Piaget and Lev Vygotsky.

Background of Jean Piaget and Lev Vygotsky

It seems quite interesting to learn that these two renowned theorists were born at the same time, although their lifespan was different and, their socio-cultural background and source of motivation were quite different; hence their diverse perception on child development.

Jean Piaget

Jean Piaget, a psychologist was born in Switzerland, in 1896 and, he is known to have possessed immense biological orientation. In his postulates, it appears evident that Piaget believed that change and transformation were the key determinants of knowledge, implying that his perspective on child development was based on operative knowledge. In other words, Piaget's constructivism perspective portrays the learning process as construction (Blake & Pope, 2008). In his investigations on students; wrong responses, Piaget identified four fundamental stages involved in cognitive development: formal, sensori-motor, concrete and pre-operational, and he explained the significant cognitive changes in each developmental stage. In regard to the sensori-motor stage, also referred to as the infancy stage, children develop knowledge through the use of the five senses and goal-directed actions and they experience an unprecedented egocentrism because; they do not incorporate other peoples' perception on their perspectives like adults. In the pre-operational stage between two and seven years of age, children develop language, and they can solve one-step logic problem. However, the element of egocentrism remains conspicuous in the child's responses. In seven to eleven years, the child shades off egocentrism and manifest substantial cognition in conversations, whereas in the formal operations stage; twelve years to adulthood, enables children to manifest logical thinking (Blake & Pope, 2008).

Le Vygotsky

Lev Vygotsky, a philosopher was born in 1896 in Russia and, he was fundamentally history and philosophy oriented. He believed that the child cognitive development was attributable to the socio-cultural environment, in which the child developed, and his investigations into the issue were greatly influenced the Marxist Theory, which states, "...historical changes in society and material life produce changes in human nature" (Blake & Pope, 2008 p. 60). He focused on the principal precepts of cognitive learning zones. In his investigations, Vygotsky designed postulates with regard to the Zone of Actual Development (ZAD) and the Zone of Proximal Development (ZPD). The Zone of Actual Development occurs when children manifest abilities to execute their tasks on their own successfully, especially at circumstances where the child does not require learning new ideas. On the other hand, the Zone of Proximal Development involves the learning of new ideas by the child; thus, assistance from peers and adults is quite essential in knowledge development (Blake & Pope, 2008). Vygotsky described the Zone of Proximal Development as the distance between the actual mental development and the potential development, especially with regard to problem-solving abilities (Fernyhough & Lloyd, 1999).

Comparison

The constructivist theories of Piagetian and Vygotskian encompass some fundamental aspects of the child cognitive development. These theories are relatively similar but, they manifest relevant differences. LeGard (2004) states, "Jean Piaget (1896-1980) and Lev Vygotsky (1896-1934) proposed the classical constructivist theories of cognitive development, although often compared; the concepts differ significantly" (p. 1). For instance, Piaget's focuses on child cognitive development with regard to time; thus, the stages are described as hierarchical in nature. As such, a child is ought to complete the stages in a sequence, in which the cognitive development begins with the sensori-motor stage and progresses to the pre-operational stage. Thereafter, the child enters the concrete stage characterized with independence in the expression of ideas followed by the formal operations stage, in which the child assumes adult thinking. It is worth noting that, in Piaget's perspective, cognitive development in children at most stages do not involve social interactions as significant elements of knowledge development. On the other hand, Vygotsky's perspective emphasizes extensively on social interactions, especially with regard to the role of assistance to the child during the developmental stages. He reported that, children acquire extensive knowledge from knowledgeable peers and adults, especially through communications and peer interaction (Slanders, 2009).

Concisely, Piaget portrayed child cognitive development as an adaptation process, in which continuous progression of accommodation and assimilation play fundamental roles in knowledge development. On the other hand, Vygotsky describes the process of cognitive development as a product of an appropriation of the child thinking pattern, in which the child learns from competent individuals during their social interactions. However, it is noting that Piaget and Vygotsky agree universally on the constructive aspect of intellectual development (LeGard, 2004).

Contrast

In regard to the principal differences between Piaget and Vygotsky, an immense contrast is manifested through numerous aspects of cognitive development and the key elements of their theories. For instance, these two theorists views the role of the child in diverse perspectives, in which Piaget places a child as a scientist, whereas, in Vygotsky's perspective, the child assumes the role of an apprentice and development is variable owing to cultural differences. Secondly, Piaget describes the learning process as a product of an individualist society but, Vygotsky describes it as the power of the community where the child is regarded to as a social being depended on the knowledge of adults and knowledgeable peers. In the perception of Piaget, cognitive development is driven by maturation and other significant aspects such as conflict (LeGard, 2004). In contrast, Vygotsky attributes cognitive development to motivation and enjoyment from the child's peers and adults.

Moreover, Piaget's and Vygotsky's perspectives differ significantly on the role of biology, language and the source of the child's cognition. Piaget believed that language development among children was driven by thought but, Vygotsky maintained that language plays the pivotal role in the child's development of ideas (LeGard, 2004). In regard to the role of biology in the child cognitive development, Piaget believed that maturation of the child correlates significantly with cognitive development, in which maturation determines the pace of cognitive development, especially with regard to the four stages of the child's development. This perception was discredited by Vygotsky who claimed that the child's elementary biological functions were innate. On the other hand, Piaget argued that the source of cognition among children is independent; that is, cognition is generated from the children themselves, contrary to Vygotsky's perception, which associated the child cognitive development to the social environment.

Another significant contrast between Piagetian and Vygotskian theories is the course of the child's cognitive development, in which Piaget argued that cognitive development declines with age, whereas Vygotsky argued that cognitive development increases significantly in youth although if declines significantly thereafter in the subsequent stages.

Conclusion

In brief conclusion, Piaget and Vygotsky exhibit significant similarities, especially with regard to their contribution to the field of the child development, although they approach the topic from different perspectives (Slanders, 2009). It appears true to assert that their differences in perception are attributable to their intellectual orientations because; they are quite different. Piaget exhibited biological orientation, whereas Vygotsky was oriented to history and philosophy with Marxist ideologies. However, it is worth acknowledging their contribution to the child development with regard to constructivist theories.

References

Blake, B. & Pope, T. (2008). Developmental Psychology: Incorporating Piaget's and Vygotsky's Theories in Classrooms. *Journal of Cross-Disciplinary Perspectives in Education, 1*(1), 59 – 67. Retrieved from http://people.wm.edu/~mxtsch/Teaching/JCPE/Volume1/JCPE_2008-01-09.pdf

Fernyhough, C. & Lloyd, P. (1999). *Lev Vygotsky. 3. The Zone of Proximal Development.* New York, NY: Routledge.

LeGard, W. (2004). *Piaget versus Vygotsky.* Retrieved from http://www.scribd.com/doc/13401568/Piaget-Versus-Vygotsky

Slanders, J. (2009). *Differences between Piaget's and Vygotsky's Theories of Development.* retrieved from http://www.personal.psu.edu/jms5355/blogs/jessicas_blog/2009/01/differences-between-piagets-and-vygotskys-theories-of-development.html

YOUR KNOWLEDGE HAS VALUE

- We will publish your bachelor's and master's thesis, essays and papers

- Your own eBook and book - sold worldwide in all relevant shops

- Earn money with each sale

Upload your text at www.GRIN.com
and publish for free

CPSIA information can be obtained
at www.ICGtesting.com
Printed in the USA
LVRC031537091120
671181LV00016B/84